D0783462

POEMS
1970–1972

ROBERT GRAVES
POEMS 1970-1972

CASSELL · LONDON

CASSELL & COMPANY LTD
35 Red Lion Square, London WC1R 4SG
Sydney, Auckland
Toronto, Johannesburg

First published 1972

I.S.B.N. 0 304 29047 5

Printed by The Camelot Press Limited,
London and Southampton
F. 772

FOREWORD

About half of these seventy-nine poems—sections XXVI and XXVII of my *Collected Poems*—have lately been published by Messrs Bertram Rota in *The Green Sailed Vessel* (1971), a signed limited edition. The series began in my *Collected Poems 1965* with eighteen sections, the first section containing a poem written as early as 1914. Section XXVI consists of love-poems; XXVII contains satire and contemporary comment.

Little need be added to my *Foreword* in *The Green Sailed Vessel*. I wrote there that, now well into my seventy-sixth year, I had become increasingly concerned with hidden powers of poetic thought, which raise and solve problems akin to those of advanced mathematics and physics. The word 'poetry' meant in Greek the 'act of making'—a sense that has survived in the old Scottish word for a poet, namely 'maker', though the Scots often spelt it *makar*. The poetic power to make things happen, as understood for instance by the early mediaeval Irish master-poets, and by their Middle Eastern Sufic contemporaries, raises simple love-alliances to a point where physical absence supplies living presence. These experiences occur not only in the fourth dimension, where prison walls are easily cheated—see the poem *A Reduced Sentence*—but in the fifth, where time proves as manipulable as is vertical or lateral space in the usual third dimension, and where seemingly impossible coincidences and so-called 'Acts of God' occur almost as a matter of course. In poetry, the fifth-dimensional coidentification of lovers is truth rather than idealistic fancy, and the phenomenon is here described—however inadequately —in *Five, Serpent's Tail, Testament, The Crab-Tree, Cliff and Wave, Three Locked Hoops* and subsequent pieces.

Recently in a broadcast I admitted my constant debt—with which I had, however, never been charged—to early Welsh prosody. In my boyhood at Harlech, North Wales, I was indoctrinated by 'Gwynedd' (the bardic name of our celebrated neighbour Canon Edwards) in *cynganedd* and other ancient metrical devices. In 1913 I even published an English *englyn* without transgressing too many of its ninety-five statutory rules. Briefly, the subsequent use I made of *cynganedd* was to strengthen my verse with complex half-concealed chains of alliteration. But I also borrowed the ancient Irish use of internal rhyme.

Prosody is now generally underrated by English and American writers, who fail to recognize it as a necessary means of hypnotizing the reader into the same dream-like mood—the top level of sleep—which the true poet himself must enter. English poetry is, I admit, complex enough without recourse to Welsh prosody; it combines the Anglo-Saxon metre of the tugged oar with the dancing metres of ancient Greece and with the resolute marching metre of the Roman legionaries—*Caesar Galliam subegit, Nicomedes Caesarem. . . .*

Deyá   R.G.
Majorca

CONTENTS

XXVI

XXVII

XXVI

THE HOOPOE TELLS US HOW

Recklessly you offered me your all,
Recklessly I accepted,
Laying my large world at your childish feet
Beyond all bounds of honourable recall:
Wild, wilful, incomplete.

Absence reintegrates our pact of pacts—
The hoopoe tells us how:
With bold love-magic, Moon in *Leo*,
Sun in *Pisces*, blossom upon bough.

THE WAND

These tears flooding my eyes, are they of pain
Or of relief: to have done with other loves,
To abstain from childish folly?

It has fallen on us to become exemplars
Of a love so far removed from gallantry
That we now meet seldom in a room apart
Or kiss goodnight, or even dine together
Unless in casual company.

For while we walk the same green paradise
And confidently ply the same green wand
That still restores the wilting hopes of others
Far more distressed than we,
How can we dread the broad and bottomless mere
Of utter infamy sunk below us
Where the eggs of hatred hatch?

FIVE

Five beringed fingers of Creation,
Five candles blazing at a shrine,
Five points of her continuous pentagram,
Five letters in her name—as five in mine.
I love, therefore I am.

QUINQUE

Quinque tibi luces vibrant in nomine: quinque
    Isidis in stella cornua sacra deae.
Nonne etiam digitos anuli quinque Isidis ornant?
    Ornant te totidem, Julia. . . . Sum, quod amo.

ARROW ON THE VANE

Suddenly, at last, the bitter wind veers round
From North-East to South-West. It is at your orders;
And the arrow on our vane swings and stays true
To your direction. Nothing parts us now.
What can I say? Nothing I have not said,
However the wind blew. I more than love,
As when you drew me bodily from the dead.

GORGON MASK

When the great ship ran madly towards the rocks
An unseen current slewed her into safety,
A dying man ashore took heart and lived,
And the moon soared overhead, ringed with three
    rainbows,
To announce the birth of a miraculous child.
Yet you preserved your silence, secretly
Nodding at me across the crowded hall.

The ship carried no cargo destined for us,
Nor were her crew or master known to us,
Nor was that sick man under our surveillance,
Nor would the child ever be born to you,
Or by me fathered on another woman—
Nevertheless our magic power ordained
These three concurrent prodigies.

Stranger things bear upon us. We are poets
Age-old in love: a full reach of desire
Would burn us both to an invisible ash. . . .
Then hide from me, if hide from me you must,
In bleak refuge among nonentities,
But wear your Gorgon mask of divine warning
That, as we first began, so must we stay.

TO BE POETS

We are two lovers of no careless breed,
Nor is our love a curiosity
(Like honey-suckle shoots from an oak tree
Or a child with two left hands) but a proud need
For royal thought and irreproachable deed;
What others write about us makes poor sense,
Theirs being a no-man's land of negligence.

To be poets confers Death on us:
Death, paradisal fiery conspectus
For those who bear themselves always as poets,
Who cannot fall beneath the ignoble curse
(Whether by love of self, whether by scorn
Of truth) never to die, never to have been born.

WITH A GIFT OF RINGS

It was no costume jewellery I sent:
True stones cool to the tongue, their settings ancient,
Their magic evident.
Conceal your pride, accept them negligently
But, naked on your couch, wear them for me.

CASSE-NOISETTE

As a scurrying snow-flake
Or a wild-rose petal
Carried by the breeze,
Dance your nightly ballet
On the set stage.

And although each scurrying
Snow-flake or rose-petal
Resembles any other—
Her established smile,
Her well-schooled carriage—

Dance to Rule, ballet-child;
Yet never laugh to Rule,
Never love to Rule!
Keep your genius hidden
By a slow rage.

So let it be your triumph
In this nightly ballet
Of snow-flakes and petals,
To present love-magic
In your single image—
With a low, final curtsey
From the set stage.

THE GARDEN

Enhanced in a tower, asleep, dreaming about him,
The twin buds of her breasts opening like flowers,
Her fingers leafed and wandering . . .
                                    Past the well
Blossoms an apple-tree, and a horde of birds
Nested in the close thickets of her hair
Grumble in dreamy dissonance,
Calling him to the garden, if he dare.

THE GREEN-SAILED VESSEL

We are like doves, well-paired,
Veering across a meadow—
Children's voices below,
Their song and echo;

Like raven, wren or crow
That cry and prophesy,
What do we not foreknow,
Whether deep or shallow?

Like the tiller and prow
Of a green-sailed vessel
Voyaging, none knows how,
Between moon and shadow;

Like the restless, endless
Blossoming of a bough,
Like tansy, violet, mallow,
Like the sun's afterglow.

Of sharp resemblances
What further must I show
Until your black eyes narrow,
Furrowing your clear brow?

DREAMING CHILDREN

They have space enough, however cramped their
    quarters,
And time enough, however short their day,
In sleep to chase each other through dream orchards
    Or bounce from rafters into buoyant hay.

But midnight thunder rolls, with frequent flashes,
    Wild hail peppers the farm-house roof and walls,
Wild wind sweeps from the North, flattening the
    bushes
    As with a crash of doom chain-lightning falls.

Split to its tap-roots, their own favourite oak-tree
    Glows like a torch across the narrow heath.
She shudders: 'Take me home again! It scares me!
    Put your arms round me, we have seen death!'

THE PROHIBITION

You were by my side, though I could not see you,
Your beauty being sucked up by the moon
In whose broad light, streaming across the valley,
We could match colours or read the finest print,
While swart tree shadows rose from living roots
Like a stockade planted against intrusion.

But since dawn spread, birds everywhere wakeful
And the sun risen masterly from the East,
Where are you now? Not standing at my side
But gone with the moon, sucked away into daylight,
All magic vanished, save for the rare instant
When a sudden arrow-shot transfixes me.

Marry into your tribe, bear noble sons
Never to call me father—which is forbidden
To poets by the laws of moon magic,
The Goddess being forever a fierce virgin
And chastening all love with prohibition
Of what her untranslatable truth transcends.

SERPENT'S TAIL

When you are old as I now am
I shall be young as you, my lamb;
For lest love's timely force should fail
The Serpent swallows his own tail.

UNTIL WE BOTH . . .

Until we both . . .
                    Strolling across Great Park
With a child and a dog, greeting the guardian lions
At the royal entrance, slowly rounding the mere
Where boats are sailed all day, this perfect Sunday,
Counting our blessings peacefully enough . . .

Until we both, at the same horrid signal,
The twelfth stroke of a clock booming behind us,
Sink through these nonchalant, broad, close-cut lawns
To a swirling no-man's land shrouded in smoke
That feeds our kisses with bright furnace embers,
And we beg anguished mercy of each other,
Exchanging vow for vow, our lips blistered . . .

Until we both . . .
                    Until we both at once . . .
Have you more courage, love, even than I
Under this final torment?
Shall we ever again greet our guardian lions
And the boats on the Great Mere?

THE ROSE

When was it that we swore to love for ever?
When did this Universe come at last to be?
The two questions are one.

Fetch me a rose from your rose-arbour
To bless this night and grant me honest sleep:
Sleep, not oblivion.

TESTAMENT

Pure melody, love without alteration,
Flame without smoke, cresses from a clean brook,
The sun and moon as it were casting dice
With ample falls of rain,
Then comes the peaceful moment of appraisal,
The first and last lines of our testament,
With you ensconced high in the castle turret,
Combing your dark hair at a silver mirror,
And me below, sharpening my quill again.

This body is now yours; therefore I own it.
Your body is now mine; therefore you own it.
As for our single heart, let it stay ours
Since neither may disown it
While still it flowers in the same dream of flowers.

THE CRAB-TREE

Because of love's infallibility,
Because of love's insistence—
And none can call us liars—
Spring heaps your lap with summer buds and flowers
And lights my mountain peaks with Beltane fires.

The sea spreads far below; its blue whale's-back
Forcing no limit on us;
We watch the boats go by
Beyond rain-laden ranks of olive trees
And, rising, sail in convoy through clear sky.

Never, yet always. Having at last perfected
Utter togetherness
We meet nightly in dream
Where no voice interrupts our confidences
Under the crab-tree by the pebbled stream.

THREE LOCKED HOOPS

Yourself, myself and our togetherness
Lock like three hoops, exempt from time and space.
Let preachers preach of sovereign trinities,
Yet can such ancient parallels concern us
Unless they too spelt He and She and Oneness?

CLIFF AND WAVE

Since first you drew my irresistible wave
To break in foam on your immovable cliff,
We occupy the same station of being—
Not as in wedlock harboured close together,
But beyond reason, co-identical.
Now when our bodies hazard an encounter,
They dread to engage the fury of their senses,
And only in the brief dismay of parting
Will your cliff shiver or my wave falter.

HER BEAUTY

Let me put on record for posterity
The uniqueness of her beauty:
Her black eyes fixed unblinking on my own,
Cascading hair, high breasts, firm nose,
Soft mouth and dancer's toes.

Which is, I grant, cautious concealment
Of a new Muse by the Immortals sent
For me to honour worthily—
Her eyes brimming with tears of more than love,
Her lips gentle, moving secretly—

And she is also the dark hidden bride
Whose beauty I invoke for lost sleep:
To last the whole night through without dreaming—
Even when waking is to wake in pain
And summon her to grant me sleep again.

ALWAYS

Slowly stroking your fingers where they lie,
Slowly parting your hair to kiss your brow—
For this will last for always (as you sigh),
Whatever follows now.

Always and always—who dares disagree
That certainty hangs upon certainty?
Yet who ever encountered anywhere
So unendurably circumstanced a pair
Clasped heart to heart under a blossoming tree
With such untamable magic of despair,
Such childlike certainty?

DESERT FRINGE

When a live flower, a single name of names,
Thrusts with firm roots into your secret heart
Let it continue ineradicably
To scent the breeze not only on her name-day
But on your own: a hedge of roses fringing
Absolute desert strewn with ancient flints
And broken shards and shells of ostrich eggs—
Where no water is found, but only sand,
And yet one day, we swear, recoverable.

THE TITLE OF POET

Poets are guardians
Of a shadowy island
With granges and forests
Warmed by the Moon.

Come back, child, come back!
You have been far away,
Housed among phantoms,
Reserving silence.

Whoever loves a poet
Continues whole-hearted,
Her other loves or loyalties
Distinct and clear.

She is young, he is old
And endures for her sake
Such fears of unease
As distance provokes.

Yet how can he warn her
What natural disasters
Will plague one who dares
To neglect her poet? . . .
For the title of poet
Comes only with death.

DEPTH OF LOVE

Since depth of love is never gauged
By proof of appetites assuaged,
Nor dare you set your body free
To take its passionate toll of me—
And with good reason—
What now remains for me to do
In proof of perfect love for you
But as I am continue,
The ecstatic bonds of monk or nun
Made odious by comparison?

BREAKFAST TABLE

Breakfast peremptorily closes
The reign of Night, her dream extravagances
Recalled for laughter only.

Yet here we sit at our own table,
Brooding apart on spells of midnight love
Long irreversible:

Spells that have locked our hearts together,
Never to falter, never again to stray
Into the fierce dichotomy of Day;
Night has a gentler laughter.

THE HALF-FINISHED LETTER

One day when I am written off as dead—
My works widely collected, rarely read
Unless as Literature (examiners
Asking each student which one he prefers
And how to classify it), my grey head
Slumped on the work-desk—they will find your name
On a half-finished letter, still the same
And in my characteristic characters:
That's one thing will have obdurately lasted.

THE HAZEL GROVE

To be well loved,
Is it not to dare all,
Is it not to do all,
Is it not to know all?
To be deep in love?

A tall red sally
Had stood for seventy
Years by the pool
(And that was plenty)
Before I could shape
My harp from her poll.

Now seven hundred
Years will be numbered
In our hazel grove
Before this vibrant
Harp falls silent—
For lack of strings,
Not for lack of love.

PITY

Sickness may seem a falling out of love,
With pleas for pity—love's lean deputy.
If so, refuse me pity, wait, love on:
Never outlaw me while I yet live.
The day may come when you too, falling sick,
Implore my pity. Let me, too, refuse it
Offering you, instead, my pitiless love.

SILENT VISIT

I was walking my garden
Judiciously, calmly,
Curved mattock in hand
Heavy basket on shoulder,
When all of a sudden

You kissed me most kindly
From forehead to chin,
Though arriving unseen
As a pledge of love-magic
And wordlessly even.

Had you come, long-announced,
Wearing velvets and silk
After travels of grandeur
From Greece to the Yemen,
Socotra and Aden.

With no rapture of silence
Nor rapture of absence—
No poem to greet you,
No burst of green glory
From trees in my garden. . . .

But you came, a grown woman,
No longer the child
Whom I loved well enough
When your age was just seven—
Who would enter alone
The close thickets of Eden
And there would run wild.

31

CORONET OF MOONLIGHT

Such was the circumstance of our first love:
Sea, silence, a full moon.
Nevertheless, even the same silence
Amended by a distant nightingale
From the same past, and gently heaving surf,
Brings me no sure revival of our dream—
For to be surely with you is to sleep,
Having well earned my coronet of moonlight
By no mere counting of processional sheep.

SONG: TO BECOME EACH OTHER

To love you truly
  I must become you,
And so to love you
  I must leave behind
All that was not you:
  All jewelled phantoms,
All fabrications
  Of a jealous mind.

For man and woman
  To become each other
Is far less hard
  Than would seem to be:
An eternal serpent
  With eyes of emerald
Stands curled around
  This blossoming tree.

Though I seem old
  As a castle turret
And you as young
  As the grass beneath
It is no great task
  To become each other
Where nothing honest
  Goes in fear of death.

HEAVEN

Laugh still, write always lovingly, for still
You neither will nor can deny your heart,
Which always was a poet's,
Even while our ways are cruelly swept apart.
But though the rose I gave you in your childhood
Has never crumbled yellowing into dust
Neither as yet have needles pricked your conscience,
Which also is a poet's,
To attempt the miracles which one day you must.

Meanwhile reject their Heaven, but guard our own
Here on this needle-point, immediately
Accessible, not sprawled like theirs across
Limitless outer space. If to those angels
We seem a million light-years yet unborn,
And cannot more concern them than they us,
Let our own Heaven, with neither choir nor throne
Nor janitor, rest inexpugnable
And private for our gentler love alone.

GROWING PAINS

My earliest love, that stabbed and lacerated,
Must I accept it as it seemed then—
Although still closely documented, dated
And even irreversibly annotated
By your own honest pen?

Love never lies, even when it most enlarges
Dimensions, griefs, or charges,
But, come what must, remains
Irrevocably true to its worst growing pains.

FRIDAY NIGHT

On the brink of sleep, stretched in a wide bed,
    Rain pattering at the windows
And proud waves booming against granite rocks:
    Such was our night of glory.

Thursday had brought us dreams only of evil,
    As the muezzin warned us:
'Forget all nightmare once the dawn breaks,
    Prepare for holy Friday!'

Friday brings dreams only of inward love
    So overpassing passion
That no lips reach to kiss, nor hands to clasp,
    Nor does foot press on foot.

We wait until the lamp has flickered out
    Leaving us in full darkness,
Each still observant of the other's lively
    Sighs of pure content.

Truth is prolonged until the grey dawn:
    Her face floating above me,
Her black hair falling cloudlike to her breasts,
    Her lovely eyes half-open.

THE PACT

The identity of opposites had linked us
In our impossible pact of only love
Which, being a man, I honoured to excess
But you, being woman, quietly disregarded—
Though loving me no less—
And, when I would have left you, envied me
My unassuageable positivity.

POOR OTHERS

Hope, not Love, twangles her single string
Monotonously and in broken rhythms.
Can Hope deserve praise?

I fell in love with you, as you with me.
Hope envies us for being otherwise
Than honest Hope should be.

No charm avails against the evil eye
Of envy but to spit into our bosoms
And so dissemble

That we are we and not such luckless others
As hope and tremble.
Shifting the blame to fathers or to mothers
For being themselves, not others:
Alas, poor others!

A TOAST TO DEATH

This is, indeed, neither the time nor the place
For victory celebrations. Victory over what?
Over Death, his grinning image and manifesto
Of which, as children, we have been forewarned
And offered a corpse's frigid hand to kiss.

Contrariwise, let me raise this unsteady glass
In a toast to Death, the sole deviser of life,
Our antenatal witness when each determined
Sex, colour, humour, religion, limit of years,
Parents, place, date of birth—
A full conspectus, with ourselves recognized
As viable capsules lodged in the fifth dimension,
Never to perish, time being irrelevant,
And the reason for which, and sole excuse, is love—
Tripled togetherness of you with me.

THE YOUNG SIBYL

The swing has its bold rhythm,
Yet a breeze in the trees
Varies the music for her
As down the apples drop
In a row on her lap.

Though still only a child
She must become our Sibyl,
A holder of the apple
Prophesying wild
Histories for her people.

Five apples in a row,
Each with ruddy cheeks,
So too her own cheeks glow
As the long swing creaks,
Pulsing to and fro.

RECORDS

Accept these records of pure love
With no end or beginning, written for
Yourself alone, not the abashed world,
Timeless therefore—

Whose exaltations clearly tell
Of a past pilgrimage through hell,
Which in the name of love I spare you.
Hell is my loneliness, not ours,
Else we should harrow it together.

Love, have you walked worse hells even than I,
Through echoing silence where no midge or fly
Buzzes—hells boundless, without change of weather?

THE FLOWERING ALOE

The century-plant has flowered, its golden blossom
Showering honey from seven times our height:
Now the stock withers fast and wonder ends.
Yet from its roots eventually will soar
Another stock to enchant your great-grandchildren
But vex my jealous, uninvited ghost,
These being no blood of mine.

CIRCUS RING

How may a lover draw two bows at once
Or ride two steeds at once,
Firm in the saddle?
Yet these are master-feats you ask of me
Who loves you crazily
When in the circus ring you rock astraddle
Your well-matched bay and grey—
Firing sharp kisses at me.

AGELESS REASON

We laugh, we frown, our fingers twitch
Nor can we yet prognosticate
How we shall learn our fate—
The occasion when, the country which—
Determined only that this season
Of royal tremulous possession
Shall find its deathless reason.

AS WHEN THE MYSTIC

To be lost for good to the gay self-esteem
That carried him through difficult years of childhood,
To be well stripped of all tattered ambitions
By his own judgement, now scorning himself
As past redemption—
                              this is anticipation
Of true felicity, as when the mystic
Starved, frightened, purged, assaulted and ignobled
Drinks Eleusinian ambrosia
From a gold cup and walks in Paradise.

UNPOSTED LETTER
(1963)

Can you still love, having once shared love's secret
With a man born to it?
Then sleep no more in graceless beds, untrue
To love, where jealousy of the secret
Will scorch away your childlike sheen of virtue—
Did he not confer crown, orb and sceptre
On a single-hearted, single-fated you?

XXVII

BIRTH OF A GODDESS

It was John the Baptist, son to Zechariah,
Who assumed the cloak of God's honest Archangel
And mouthpiece born on Monday, Gabriel,
And coming where his cousin Mary span
Her purple thread or stitched a golden tassel
For the curtain of the Temple Sanctuary,
Hailed her as imminent mother, not as bride—
Leaving the honest virgin mystified.

Nor would it be a man-child she must bear:
Foreseen by John as a Messiah sentenced
To ransom all mankind from endless shame—
But a Virgin Goddess cast in her own image
And bearing the same name.

BEATRICE AND DANTE

He, a grave poet, fell in love with her.
She, a mere child, fell deep in love with love
And, being a child, illumined his whole heart.

From her clear conspect rose a whispering
With no hard words in innocency held back—
Until the day that she became woman,

Frowning to find her love imposed upon:
A new world beaten out in her own image—
For his own deathless glory.

THE DILEMMA

Tom Noddy's body speaks, not so his mind;
  Or his mind speaks, not so Tom Noddy's body.
Undualistic truth is hard to find
  For the distressed Tom Noddy.

Mind wanders blindly, body misbehaves;
  Body sickens, mind at last repents,
Each calling on the heart, the heart that saves,
  Disposes, glows, relents.

Which of these two must poor Tom's heart obey:
  The mind seduced by logical excess
To misbehaviour, or its lonely prey—
  The unthinking body sunk in lovelessness?

THE GENTLEMAN

That he knows more of love than you, by far,
And suffers more, has long been his illusion.
His faults, he hopes, are few—maybe they are
With a life barred against common confusion;
But that he knows far less and suffers less,
Protected by his age, his reputation,
His gentlemanly sanctimoniousness,
Has blinded him to the dumb grief that lies
Warring with love of love in your young eyes.

THE WALL

A towering wall divides your house from mine.
You alone hold the key to the hidden door
That gives you secret passage, north to south,
Changing unrecognizably as you go.
The south side borders on my cherry orchard
Which, when you see, you smile upon and bless.
The north side I am never allowed to visit;
Your northern self I must not even greet,
Nor would you welcome me if I stole through.

I have a single self, which never alters
And which you love more than the whole world
Though you fetch nothing for me from the north
And can bring nothing back. To be a poet
Is to have no wall parting his domain,
Never to change. Whenever you stand by me
You are the Queen of poets, and my judge.
Yet you return to play the Mameluke
Speaking a language alien to our own.

WOMEN AND MASKS

Translated from Gabor Devesceri's Hungarian

Women and masks: an old familiar story.
Life slowly drains away and we are left
As masks of what we were. The living past
Rightly respects all countenances offered
As visible sacrifices to the gods
And clamps them fast even upon live faces.
Let face be mask then, or let mask be face—
Mankind can take its ease, may assume godhead.
Thus God from time to time descends in power
Graciously, not to a theologian's hell
But to our human hell enlaced with heaven.

Let us wear masks once worn in the swift circlings
And constant clamour of a holy dance
Performed always in prayer, in the ecstasy
Of love-hate murder—today's children always
Feeling, recording, never understanding.

Yet this old woman understands, it seems,
At least the unimportance of half-knowledge,
Her face already become mask, her teeth
Wide-gapped as though to scare us, her calm face
Patterned with wrinkles in unchanging grooves
That outlive years, decades and centuries.
Hers is a mask remains exemplary
For countless generations. Who may wear it?
She only, having fashioned it herself.
So long as memory lasts us, it was hers.

Behind it she assembles her rapt goodness,
Her gentle worth already overflooding
The mask, her prison, shaming its fierce, holy
Terror: for through its gaping sockets always
Peer out a pair of young and lovely eyes.

TILTH

('Robert Graves, the British veteran, is no longer in the poetic swim. He still resorts to traditional metres and rhyme, and to such out-dated words as *tilth*; withholding his 100% approbation also from contemporary poems that favour sexual freedom.'

From a New York critical weekly)

Gone are the drab monosyllabic days
When 'agricultural labour' still was *tilth*;
And '100% approbation', *praise*;
And 'pornographic modernism', *filth*—
Yet still I stand by *tilth* and *filth* and *praise*.

THE LAST FISTFUL

He won her Classic races, at the start,
With a sound wind, strong legs and gallant heart;
Yet she reduced his fodder day by day
Till she had sneaked the last fistful away—
When, not unnaturally, the old nag died
Leaving her four worn horseshoes and his hide.

THE TRADITIONALIST

Respect his obstinacy of undefeat,
His hoarding of tradition,
Those hands hung loosely at his side
Always prepared for hardening into fists
Should any fool waylay him,
His feet prepared for the conquest of crags
Or a week's march to the sea.

If miracles are recorded in his presence
As in your own, remember
These are no more than time's obliquities
Gifted to men who still fall deep in love
With real women like you.

THE PREPARED STATEMENT

The Prepared Statement is a sure stand-by
For business men and Ministers. A lie
Blurted by thieves caught in the very act
Shows less regard, no doubt, for the act's fact
But more for truth; and all good thieves know why.

ST ANTONY OF PADUA

Love, when you lost your keepsake,
The green-eyed silver serpent,
And called upon St Antony
   To fetch it back again,
The fact was that such keepsakes
Must never become idols
And meddle with the magic
   That chains us with its chain:
Indeed the tears it cost you
By sliding from your finger
Was Antony's admonishment
   That magic must remain
Dependent on no silver ring
Nor serpent's emerald eyes
But equally unalterable,
   Acceptable and plain . . .
Yet none the less St Antony
(A blessing on his honesty!)
Proved merciful to you and me
   And found that ring again.

BROKEN COMPACT

It was not he who broke their compact;
But neither had he dared to warn her
How dangerous was the act.
It might have seemed cruel blackmail,
Not mere foreknowledge, to confess
What powers protected and supported him
In his mute call for singleheartedness.

It was she indeed who planted the first kiss,
Pleading with him for true togetherness—
Therefore her faults might well be charged against
    him.
She dared to act as he had never dared.
Nor could he change: his heart remaining full,
Commanded by her, yet unconquerable,
Blinding her with its truth.
                  So, worse than blind,
He suffered more than she in body and mind.

A DREAM OF
FRANCES SPEEDWELL

I fell in love at my first evening party.
You were tall and fair, just seventeen perhaps,
Talking to my two sisters. I kept silent
And never since have loved a tall fair girl,
Until last night in the small windy hours
When, floating up an unfamiliar staircase
And into someone's bedroom, there I found her
Posted beside the window in half-light
Wearing that same white dress with lacy sleeves.
She beckoned. I came closer. We embraced
Inseparably until the dream faded.
Her eyes shone clear and blue. . . .

Who was it, though, impersonated you?

THE ENCOUNTER

Von Masoch met the Count de Sade
    In Hell as he strode by.
'Pray thrash me soundly, Count!' he begged.
    His lordship made reply:

'What? Strike a lacquey who *enjoys*
    Great blows that bruise and scar?'
'I love you, Count,' von Masoch sighed,
    'So cruel to me you are.'

AGE GAP

My grandfather, who blessed me as a child
Shortly before the Diamond Jubilee,
Was born close to the date of Badajoz
And I have grandchildren well past your age—
One married, with a child, expecting more.

How prudently you chose to be a girl
And I to be a boy! Contrary options
Would have denied us this idyllic friendship—
Boys never fall in love with great-grandmothers.

NIGHTMARE OF SENILITY

Then must I punish you with trustfulness
Since you can trust yourself no more and dread
Fresh promptings to deceive me? Or instead
Must I reward you by deceiving you,
By heaping coals of fire on my own head?
Are truth and friendship dead?

And why must I, turning in nightmare on you,
Bawl out my lies as though to make them true?
O if this Now were once, when pitifully
You dressed my wounds, kissed and made much of me,
Though warned how things must be!
    *   *   *   *   *   *

Very well, then: my head across the block,
A smile on your pursed lips, and the axe poised
For a merciful descent. Ministering to you
Even in my torment, praising your firm wrists,
Your resolute stance. . . . How else can I protect you
From the curse my death must carry, except only
By begging you not to prolong my pain
Beyond these trivial years?
                         I am young again.
I watch you shrinking to a wrinkled hag.
Your kisses grow repulsive, your feet shuffle
And drag. Now I forget your name and forget mine . . .
No matter, they were always equally 'darling'.
Nor were my poems lies; you made them so
To mystify our friends and our friends' friends.
We were the loveliest pair: all-powerful too,
Until you came to loathe me for the hush
That our archaic legend forced on you.

RESEARCH AND DEVELOPMENT:
CLASSIFIED

We reckon Cooke our best chemist alive
And therefore the least certain to survive
Even by crediting his way-out findings
To our Department boss, Sir Bonehead Clive.

Those Goblins, guessing which of us is what
(And, but for Cooke, we're far from a bright lot),
Must either pinch his know-how or else wipe him.
He boasts himself quite safe. By God, he's not!

In fact, we all conclude that Cooke's one hope
Is neither loud heroics nor soft soap:
Cooke must defect, we warn him, to the Goblins,
Though even they may grudge him enough rope.

FOOLS

There is no fool like an old fool,
  Yet fools of middling age
Can seldom teach themselves to reach
  True folly's final stage.

Their course of love mounts not above
  Some five-and-forty years,
Though God gave men threescore and ten
  To scald with foolish tears.

.

THOSE BLIND FROM BIRTH

Those blind from birth ignore the false perspective
Of those who see. Their inward-gazing eyes
Broaden or narrow no right-angle;
Nor does a far-off mansion fade for them
To match-box size.

Those blind from birth live by their four sound senses.
Only a fool disguises voice and face
When visiting the blind. Smell, tread and hand-clasp
Announce just why, and in what mood, he visits
That all-observant place.

THE GATEWAY

After three years of constant courtship
Each owes the other more than can be paid
Short of a single bankruptcy.
                              Both falter
At the gateway of the garden; each advances
One foot across it, hating to forgo
The pangs of womanhood and manhood;
Both turn about, breathing love's honest name,
Too strictly tied by bonds of miracle
And lasting magic to be easily lured
Into acceptance of concubinage:
Its deep defraudment of their regal selves.

69

ADVICE FROM A MOTHER

Be advised by me, darling:
If you hope to keep my love,
Do not marry that man!

I cannot be mistaken:
There is murder on his conscience
And fear in his heart.

I knew his grandparents:
The stock is good enough,
Clear of criminal taint.

And I find no vice in him,
Only a broken spirit
Which the years cannot heal;

And gather that, when younger,
He volunteered for service
With a secret police;

That one day he had orders
From a number and a letter
Which had to be obeyed,

And still cannot confess,
In fear for his own life,
Nor make reparation.

The dead in their bunkers
Call to him every night:
'Come breakfast with us!'

70

No gentleness, no love,
Can cure a broken spirit;
I forbid you to try.

A REDUCED SENTENCE

They were confused at first, being well warned
That the Governor forbade, by a strict rule,
All conversation between long-term prisoners—
Except cell-mates (who were his own choice);
Also, in that mixed prison, the two sexes
Might catch no glimpse whatever of each other
Even at fire-drill, even at Church Service.

Yet soon—a most unusual case—this pair
Defied the spirit, although not the letter,
Of his harsh rules, using the fourth dimension
For passage through stone walls and cast-iron doors
As coolly as one strolls across Hyde Park:
Bringing each other presents, kisses, news.

By good behaviour they reduced their sentence
From life to a few years, then out they went
Through three-dimensional gates, gently embraced . . .
And walked away together, arm in arm. . . .
But, home at last, halted abashed and shaking
Where the stairs mounted to a double bed.

ABSENT CRUSADER

An ancient rule prescribed for true knights
Was: 'Never share your couch with a true lady
Whom you would not care in honour to acknowledge
As closest to your heart, on whose pure body
You most would glory to beget children
And acknowledge them your own.'

The converse to which rule, for fine ladies,
No knight could preach with firm authority;
Nor could he venture to condemn any
Who broke the rule even while still sharing
Oaths of love-magic with her absent knight,
Telling herself: 'This is not love, but medicine
For my starved animal body; and my right.
Such peccadilloes all crusades afford—
As when I yield to my own wedded Lord.'

COMPLAINT AND REPLY

I

After our death, when scholars try
To arrange our letters in due sequence,
No one will envy them their task,
You sign you name so lovingly
So sweetly and so neatly
That all must be confounded by
Your curious reluctance,
Throughout this correspondence,
To answer anything I ask
Though phrased with perfect prudence . . .
Why do you wear so blank a mask,
Why always baulk at a reply
Both in and out of sequence,
Yet sign your name so lovingly,
So sweetly and so neatly?

II

Oh, the dark future! I confess
Compassion for your scholars—yes.
Not being myself incorrigible,
Trying most gallantly, indeed,
To answer what I cannot read,
With half your words illegible
Or, at least, any scholar's guess.

MY GHOST

I held a poor opinion of myself
When young, but never bettered my opinion
(Even by comparison)
Of all my fellow-fools at school or college.

Passage of years induced a tolerance,
Even a near-affection, for myself—
Which, when you fell in love with me, amounted
(Though with my tongue kept resolutely tied)
To little short of pride.

Pride brought its punishment: thus to be haunted
By my own ghost whom, much to my disquiet,
All would-be friends and open enemies
Boldly identified and certified
As me, including him in anecdotal
Autobiographies.

Love, should you meet him in the newspapers
In planes, on trains, or at large get-togethers,
I charge you, disregard his foolish capers;
Silence him with a cold unwinking stare
Where he sits opposite you at table
And let all present watch amazed, remarking
On how little you care.

SONG: RECONCILIATION

The storm is done, the sun shines out,
  The blackbird calls again
With bushes, trees and long hedgerows
  Still twinkling bright with rain.

Sweet, since you now can trust your heart
  As surely as I can,
Be still the sole woman I love
  With me for your sole man.

For though we hurt each other once
  In youthful blindness, yet
A man must learn how to forgive
  What women soon forget.

KNOBS AND LEVERS

Before God died, shot while running away,
He left mankind His massive hoards of gold:
Which the Devil presently appropriated
With the approval of all major trusts
As credit for inhumanizable
Master-machines and adequate spare-parts.

Men, born no longer in God's holy image,
Were graded as ancillary knobs or levers
With no Law to revere nor faith to cherish.
'You are free, Citizens,' old Satan crowed;
And all felicitated one another
As quit of patriarchal interference.

This page turns slowly: its last paragraph
Hints at a full-scale break-down implemented
By famine and disease. Nevertheless
The book itself runs on for five more chapters.
God died; clearly the Devil must have followed.
But was there not a Goddess too, God's mother?

THE VIRUS

We can do little for these living dead
Unless to help them bury one another
By an escalation of intense noise
And the logic of computers.
They are, we recognize, past praying for—
Only among the moribund or dying
Is treatment practical.

Faithfully we experiment, assuming
That death is a still undetected virus
And most contagious where
Men eat, smoke, drink and sleep money:
Its monstrous and unconscionable source.

DRUID LOVE

No Druid can control a woman's longing
Even while dismally foreboding
Death for her lover, anguish for herself
Because of bribes accepted, pledges broken,
Breaches hidden.
              More than this, the Druid
May use no comminatory incantations
Against either the woman or her lover,
Nor ask what punishment she herself elects.

But if the woman be herself a Druid?
The case worsens: he must flee the land.
Hers is a violence unassessable
Save by herself—ultimate proof and fury
Of magic power, dispelling all restraint
That princely laws impose on those who love.

PROBLEMS OF GENDER

Circling the Sun, at a respectful distance,
Earth remains warmed, not roasted; but the Moon
Circling the Earth, at a disdainful distance,
Will drive men lunatic (should they defy her)
With seeds of wintry love, not sown for spite.

Mankind, so far, continues undecided
On the Sun's gender—grammars disagree—
As on the Moon's. Should Moon be god, or goddess:
Drawing the tide, shepherding flocks of stars
That never show themselves by broad daylight?

Thus curious problems of propriety
Challenge all ardent lovers of each sex:
Which circles which at a respectful distance,
Or which, instead, at a disdainful distance?
And who controls the regal powers of night?

JUS PRIMAE NOCTIS

Love is a game for only two to play at,
Nor could she banish him from her soft bed
Even on her bridal night, *jus primae noctis*
Being irreversibly his. He took the wall-side
Long ago granted him. Her first-born son
Would claim his name, likeness and character.
Nor did we ask her why. The case was clear:
Even though that lover had been nine years dead
She could not banish him from her soft bed.

CONFESS, MARPESSA

Confess, Marpessa, who is your new lover?
Could he be, perhaps, that skilful rough-sea diver
Plunging deep in the waves, curving far under
Yet surfacing at last with controlled breath?

Confess, Marpessa, who is your new lover?
Is he some ghoul, with naked greed of plunder
Urging his steed across the gulf of death,
A brood of dragons tangled close beneath?

Or could he be the fabulous Salamander,
Courting you with soft flame and gentle ember?
Confess, Marpessa, who is your new lover?

DREAM RECALLED ON WAKING

The monstrous and three-headed cur
Rose hugely when she stroked his fur,
Using his metapontine tail
To lift her high across the pale.

Ranging those ridges far and near
Brought blushes to her cheek, I fear,
Yet who but she, the last and first
Could dare what lions never durst?

Proud Queen, continue as you are,
More steadfast than the Polar Star,
Yet still pretend a child to be
Gathering sea-wrack by the sea.

WORK DRAFTS

I am working at a poem, pray excuse me,
Which may take twenty drafts or more to write
Before tomorrow night,
But since no poem should be classed with prose,
I must not call it 'work', God knows—
Again, excuse me!

My poem (or non-poem) will come out
In the *New Statesman* first, no doubt,
And in hard covers gradually become
A handsome source of supplementary income,
Selected for *Great Poems*—watch the lists—
And by all subsequent anthologists.

Poems are not, we know, composed for money
And yet my work (or play)-drafts carefully
Hatched and cross-hatched by puzzling layers of ink
Are not the detritus that you might think:
They fetch from ten to fifty bucks apiece
In sale to Old Gold College Library
Where swans, however black, are never geese—
Excuse me and excuse me, pray excuse me!

COLOPHON

Dutifully I close this book. . . .
Its final pages, with the proud look
Of timelessness that your love lends it,
Call only for a simple Colophon
(Rose, key or shepherd's crook)
To announce it as your own
Whose coming made it and whose kiss ends it.